Let's Talk About
Having Allergies

Elizabeth Weitzman

The Rosen Publishing Group's
PowerKids Press™
New York

Published in 1997 by The Rosen Publishing Group, Inc.
29 East 21st Street, New York, NY 10010

First Edition

Book Design: Erin McKenna

Photo Illustrations: Cover by Carrie Ann Grippo; p. 4 © Dusty Williams/International Stock; all other photo illustrations by Seth Dinnerman.

Weitzman, Elizabeth.
    Let's talk about having allergies / Elizabeth Weitzman.
        p.   cm. —— (The let's talk library)
    Includes index.
    Summary: Briefly discusses different types of allergies, causes of allergic reactions, and treatments.
    ISBN 0-8239-5033-6
    1. Allergy——Juvenile literature. [1. Allergy.] I. Title. II. Series.
    RC584.W45 1996
    616.97–dc20
                                                                                    96-18004
                                                                                    CIP
                                                                                    AC

Manufactured in the United States of America

Table of Contents

Tamara

When Tamara was seven, her dad brought home a big surprise: a puppy. Tamara took good care of her new pet. She fed him before she left for school and played with him every day.

But after a few weeks, her mom noticed that Tamara was sick all the time. She was always sneezing, and her eyes were watering a lot. Tamara thought she just had a cold. But she was **allergic** (uh-LER-jik) to her new puppy.

◀ People can be allergic to different kinds of things, such as cats or dogs.

What Is an Allergy?

An **allergy** (AL-er-jee) is your body's **reaction** (ree-AK-shun) to a certain thing. Some people don't have any allergies at all. But other people have a list of things that they are allergic to. For many people, puppies are fun to play with. But Tamara's body is not able to be around dogs. Sneezes, watery eyes, and itchy skin are her body's way of telling her that dogs are on her "bad list."

Your body has ways of telling ▶ you that you have an allergy.

Allergens

Anything that causes an allergy is called an **allergen** (AL-er-jen). People can be allergic to almost anything. Some people are allergic to foods, like chocolate or peanuts. Others have allergies to certain **medicines** (MED-ih-sinz), such as aspirin. Sometimes allergens are found in nature—many people are allergic to flowers or bee stings. You may be allergic to only one thing. Or you may have a bad reaction to many things.

◀ Milk, chocolate, and flowers are some examples of allergens.

Are You Allergic?

Your body has ways of telling you if it doesn't like something. Your eyes may get watery around your neighbor's dog. If you're allergic to poison ivy, you'll get a rash after you touch it.

Remember, coughing or sneezing doesn't always mean you have an allergy. You might just have a cold. But if you always sneeze around dogs, you're probably allergic to them.

If you sneeze a lot around dogs, ▶
you may be allergic to them.

How Do You Know for Sure?

There's only one way to know for sure if you have an allergy. You have to visit a doctor. There are certain doctors who know all about allergies. Your parents will probably take you to see one. First, the doctor will ask you questions about your "bad list." Then she'll test your skin, usually by pricking it or putting a sticky patch on it. This will tell her what your body is allergic to.

◀ The doctor can help you figure out if you have an allergy.

How Do You Get Allergies?

Allergies are not like the flu. You can't catch them from other people. Most of the time, they are passed down from one or both of your parents. This means that you were born with allergies, just like you were born with the same blue eyes or brown hair as your dad. Of course, you may not have allergies even if a parent does. And even if you do have them, they might not be the same as your mom's or dad's.

Even though you and your mom have allergies, you may be allergic to different things. ▶

Be a Detective

There are many things you can do to make your allergies easier to live with. The best thing to do is to try and stay away from your allergens. If you're allergic to corn, that means you shouldn't eat corn on the cob, popcorn, or foods cooked in corn oil. So you have to be a **detective** (deh-TEKT-iv). Check the labels on food. Don't be afraid to ask about certain foods in restaurants. This might feel funny at first, but you'll get used to it.

◄ It's a good idea to avoid foods that you are allergic to.

If You Can't Avoid Your Allergens

Some people are allergic to things we can't see, such as dust or the **pollen** (POL-in) that blows in the air. These people usually take medicine for their allergies. They might take a special pill every day, or go to the doctor for weekly shots. Some people just take medicine when they have a bad reaction. A bad reaction to an allergen is also called an allergy attack.

Shots can help keep your allergies from bothering you. ▶

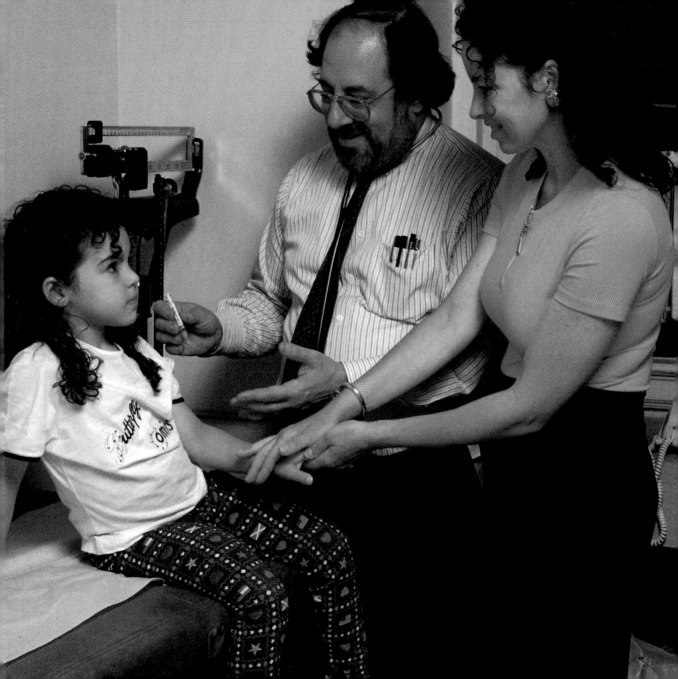

Always Be Prepared

If you have allergies, you always have to be prepared. You never know when you'll meet an allergen! So always make sure your parents, teachers, and the school nurse have your medicine handy. This may seem silly at first. For example, if you're allergic to wasps, you could go a whole summer without even seeing one. But what if you do get stung? You'll want to take your medicine as quickly as you can.

Knowing your allergens will help you be ready when you are around one.

Living with Your Allergies

Sometimes allergies get worse as people get older. Other times, they won't be as bad, or they might even go away. There's no way to know what will happen with your allergies. But one thing is for sure—the better you are at being a detective, the easier it will be to avoid your allergens. If you can watch out for them, and take your medicine when you're supposed to, you'll find that allergies are a lot easier to live with.

Glossary

allergen (AL-er-jen) Something that causes an allergic reaction.

allergic (uh-LER-jik) Having a bad reaction to something that is usually harmless.

allergy (AL-er-jee) A bad reaction to a usually harmless thing.

detective (deh-TEKT-iv) A person who learns the facts about something.

medicine (MED-ih-sin) A chemical that helps your body.

pollen (POL-in) Fine powder that comes from certain flowers and plants.

reaction (ree-AK-shun) A response to something.

Index